SNOWBOARDERS START-UP!

A Beginner's Guide
to Snowboarding

SNOWBOARDERS START-UP!

A Beginner's Guide
to Snowboarding

Doug Werner

Pathfinder Publishing of California
Ventura, California

SNOWBOARDER'S START-UP

By
Doug Werner

Published by:
Pathfinder Publishing of California
458 Dorothy Avenue
Ventura, CA 93003
(805) 642-9278

Library of Congress Cataloging-in-Publication Data

Werner, Doug.   1950–
    Snowboarder's start-up : a beginner's guide to snowboarding / by Doug Werner.
        p.   cm.
    Includes index.
    ISBN   0-934793-53-0 ; $9.95
    1. Snowboarding.   I. Title.
GV857 .S57W47   1993
796.9—dc20

93-30926
CIP

To

EUGENE WHEELER

ACKNOWLEDGMENTS

A passel of folks are to be thanked for 1001 reasons:

Kathleen Wheeler
Eugenie Wheeler
Eugene Werner
Ann Werner
Stu Kenson
Robin Niehaus
Craig McClain
Snow Valley Ski Resort
Kevin Kinnear — *TransWorld SNOWboarding* Magazine
Lee Crane—*TransWorld SNOWboarding* Magazine
Henry Hester—Lib Tech and Gnu Snowboards
Dan Poynter
Jacki DiFilippo—Burton Snowboards
David Schriber—Burton Snowboards
Jake Burton Carpenter — Burton Snowboards

Ted Martin— International Snowboard Federation (ISF)
Margi La Porte
Jim Montalbano
Mika
Marta Meler
Tamara Parsons
Squaw Valley Ski Resort
Mark Suchomel
Larry Block
Todd Huber
Carol Weidman
Vern Weidman
Tom Sims—Sims Snowboards
Jana Thompson—*The Orange County Register*
Chris Bachman—Shred Shop
Veronique de Turenne — *Daily News*
Leah Malloy
Cheryl Haab

PREFACE

Ask a snowboarder what his or her greatest difficulty was in learning how to snowboard and the reply will probably be, "My first day!" Every snowboarder I know has a sad tale to tell about their first time strapped to a slippery board.

And I was no different. My first experience was a disaster. Man, I got so trashed I thought I'd never go back!

My second day, however, was a complete turnaround. With the help of proper instruction and a PLAN, I managed to put together some turns and had a decent ride or two. I was hooked! When I got home I booked a flight to Reno and spent the next 10 days at Squaw Valley.

Snowboarder's Start-Up includes that same 'plan' of instruction which worked so well for me and my snowboarding buddies. The book is light, easy to read and loaded with photos. Hopefully it'll help get you through that first day or two with a sense of direction and discovery.

Anyway, enjoy the book, have fun up there, and stick with it!

Doug Werner

GOOD ADVICE

The sport you have chosen to learn is rapidly becoming the most popular, intense, and fun activity in the mountains today. Millions enjoy snowboarding at ski areas worldwide and the upside is practically limitless.

But.

Although carving down the slopes seems so natural now, it wasn't so long ago that so many had to fight tooth and nail to acquire the PRIVILEGE to snowboard at ski resorts.

That's right. Privilege.

You see, ski areas are empowered to allow or ban snowboarding as they see fit. It is NOT an inalienable right. Every time some Barney (or Barnette) among us ignores basic rules of safety and endangers him/herself and/or others, our privilege is in jeopardy.

So as you learn to slide, learn how to do so safely and with consideration for ALL others using the slopes. Chapters 7 and 8 cover this stuff well. READ THEM!

By the way, you will discover that being adequately safe and considerate will not impede your fun, style, or attitude unless you're criminally insane. It just may, however, prevent broken body syndrome. And promote a little goodwill.

The power to positively promote snowboarding ultimately lies with YOU. You are our representative on the slopes. Not this book, or the magazines, or the videos, or the TV programs. Carry yourself with respect and give it out. The payback is open slopes and a flourishing sport.

Anyway . . .

Welcome to the sport! Do it and have lotsa fun. But do it right, do it safe, and do it with an attitude. As in globally harmonious.

TED MARTIN
International Snowboard Federation (ISF)

CONTENTS

INTRODUCTION

MY METHOD

This book is a place to begin. Hopefully, it will get you excited about a terrific new sport. It's what I call 'beginner-friendly.' That is, I assume that you, the reader, have never skied before or even been in the mountains, for that matter. Everyone is a total civilian and needs instructions in big letters from A to Z. This is not out of arrogance on my part. Actually, it's how I like to be taught anything new myself. Very, very simply. Step by step by step.

This is not a substitute for instruction. I strongly recommend real live instruction. This is a supplemental resource where it is all written down. A reference.

And I certainly don't guarantee you'll be shredding (not even close!) after you read this. Only that you'll probably give it a try. Safely, with a sense of direction and hopefully, amusement. Because after all, snowboarding is all about having fun.

TELLING STATS

Hotbeds of snowboarding activity across the nation report significant numbers for the 1993 season. Snowboarders accounted for up to 65% of early season lift ticket sales and 10–20% overall. Projected figures for the year 2000 indicate that 28% of the mountain sliders across the USA (that's 4,783,000) will be snowboarders.

Perhaps the most telling numbers are in the 12–20 year old age group. Resorts are reporting that of the learners in this group, nearly 75% are picking up snowboarding versus skiing. The kids wanna shred!

Now stats are stats but it's clear that snowboarding is not a fad, that young folks are calling it their own and more and more greyheads (like me) have been seen streaking on a slat.

MYTHOLOGY

The wild man image of snowboarding reminds me of bygone surfing days when that sport was very young. Surfing was a real rebel's activity, or so went the image. Young punks sneering at convention in style, manner and attitude. Surfers had long, unkempt hair before the Rolling Stones. And that was before ANYBODY since Sitting Bull and Buffalo Bill. Yeah, surfers were the ones parents of sweet young children were absolutely terrified of.

Now look at surfing. It's just like rock 'n' roll. Parents dig it too. It's mainstream because surfers grew up and kept surfing. And became mommies and daddies, breadwinners, mortgage holders, and just plain older folks. Oh sure, there's a radical element, but the sport itself is totally respectable. Who woulda thunk it in 1963? And snowboarding will follow suit in its own fashion. Probably in a lot bigger way, because there's more room for snowboarding to grow.

First of all, underneath all the image stuff is a dynamite, legitimate sport. Without a doubt. Second, more people can and will do it because there are mountains inland. It's accessible to the masses. Like skiing. Also, snowboarding conditions are more predictable and sustainable than surfing conditions, which are absolutely unpredictable outside of wave pools.

The sport is on the verge of being monster, hence Big Business, hence mainstream. Like skiing. Actually, it's probably already happened. I mean all that real bad boy stuff is ten years old. Face it, shredders — there's too many of you now to be mere rebels. Or even a new wave.

And take note, skiers. These snowboarder types are here to stay. Because their sport is just as cool as yours.

GETTING ALONG

Snowboarders and skiers had a much rockier relationship a few years ago, before the legitimacy of snowboarding dawned on everybody. The sport was new, adventurous and irksome to those who didn't want any new adventures around them. It didn't help matters that the first waves of snowboarders were long on enthusiasm but short on skills. These new adventurers were deemed dangerous. Also young, rowdy and . . . different. Snowboarding was banned from a lot of places.

As time went by, the learning curve among the early boarders shot up. The newer waves of snowboarders had skills to emulate. There was less winging it and more instruction. In general, the skill level rose and with it greater and greater acceptance. At the same time the sport's popularity began to soar. Most major ski areas are now open to snowboarding or at least considering it. How could they not? That would be a heck of a lot of business to turn down.

Sure, there's still some conflict, but it's superficial. Like not liking each other's clothing. Or colors. Or language. Or age.

Big Business will take care of that. As well as the greatest healer of all: Time. Ski areas will cater to both because both want to buy lift tickets. Skiers and snowboarders will simply have to learn to live with each other. And as everybody gets older the grounds for conflict will be forgotten. Or joked about. Like Beatle haircuts.

And then something else will arrive on the scene to rattle everyone's cage!

MY APOLOGIES

#1 Snowboarding is not a male-only activity. There are plenty of HOT female riders around, believe me. Unfortunately my book has a lotta photos of just one guy demonstrating technique. I wanted to include a woman as well but time and logistics worked against that happening. I'm sorry about that because it does not reflect how I feel about where this sport is going. The greatest thing that has happened in the mountains in 50 years is open to the entire public. Regardless of age, sex, political affiliation or shoe size.

#2 Snowboarding design and engineering is a wonderous and constantly evolving thing. Among the leading manufacturers, the technology is like something out of NASA. My sketchy descriptions of equipment do no justice to the innovations being made as I write. I'm just describing what I encountered and what you will probably encounter in the rental shops.

The sport can be said to be a great and growing one for three reasons:

1) It just is!

2) Talented riders push the limits every day.

3) Gifted minds are creating ever better tools with which to ride faster, safer, and more creatively.

WHAT IS SNOWBOARDING?

SNOW

Snow happens in mountains and can provide a suitable base for snowboarding anywhere from December through April in the northern hemisphere. The season is longer or shorter depending on altitude, location, and specific weather conditions. The season is reversed (June to October) in the southern hemisphere.

Chances are your first forays onto the slopes will be in ski areas. Places that have runs or ski trails carved into the mountains with ski lifts, bars, restaurants, rental shops, ski schools, gift shops, etc., etc. As opposed to out in the back country somewhere. In established ski areas, the snow is groomed, and even made by machines. Each day, grooming is done by big, specially made machines with large caterpillar tracks that press down fresh snow into a firm surface. They also eliminate bumps, spread the snow evenly and fill in dips. These 'snocats' also break up crusted or icy snow.

Snow-making machines make real snow by blasting out an air/water mixture at tremendous pressure that breaks up the water molecules. These broken molecules freeze into crystals before they land. Obviously, Nature must supply the freezing weather. Artificial snow-making extends the season for those areas with little snowfall.

Because of these modern innovations, by and large a ski area will have decent snow for snowboarding, unless: 1) it's so early or late in the season that snow cover is poor (exposed earth, rocks, etc.), 2) warm weather during the day has turned snow into slush, or 3) cold weather has turned slushy snow into ice. You can't learn to snowboard on dirt or ice. Slush isn't a whole lot better. Before making any trip to the mountains, call ahead for snow conditions.

BOARDING

Snowboards are usually made of laminated fibreglass and wood. They're starting to come out with a lot of different shapes, but for sure the nose of the thing curves up, like a ski. There is a binding for each foot, and they are adjustable. One wears a special boot for this activity that provides necessary foot and ankle support. This sport is all about strapping yourself onto one of these things and zooming down snow covered hills and mountains.

PHYSICS (Just a Little)

This stuff can get real involved, so we'll keep it simple. You're going to learn how to slide down a hill on a snowboard. Gravity will pull you down on the

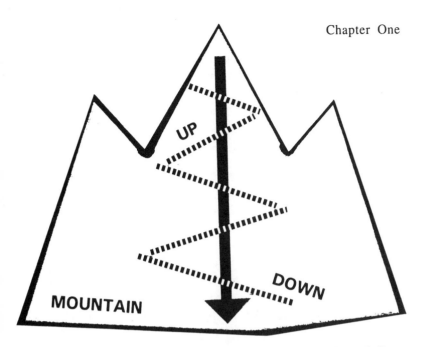

The arrow indicates the **fall line** and the dotted line indicates a **traversing** path through it.

plane of your snowboard. If you don't do a thing but stand so that the snowboard is flat on the slope, you will naturally hurtle straight down the path of least resistance. This is called the *fall line*. If you let a ball roll down the face of the hill, it would take this path.

Now. Since shooting the fall line is akin to jumping out of an airplane without a parachute, it's important to learn how to turn back and forth across the fall line. This is how you control your speed and your descent. Making a move to cross the fall line and slow down is called *traversing*.

Turning involves working in concert with the edges of your board. The edges are the sides of the snowboard. Turns happen when one of your two edges dig into the snow, creating resistance. Your body is pushed around this deflection, and you change direction.

Mastering the methods of working with the edges of your snowboard is the key to controlling your downhill flight. Knowing when and how to move from edge to edge, in and out of the fall line, is the essence of downhill snowboarding. EDGES RULE!

SNOCATS AND SNOWBOARDING PIONEERS

Way back in 1979, a cadre of snowboarders managed to convince the powers at the Fairfield Snowbowl in Arizona to allow snowboarding. Understand back then that snowboarding was REALLY NEW and REALLY DIFFERENT. And something to be suspicious of. Snowboarders could use the mountain only if they got on and off the lifts with some sort of skis. There was a question of control. The skis of choice were three-foot plastic models from the Goodwill.

Anyway, within a month a snowboarder got into a fight with the ski patrol and the thread of tolerance was broken. Snowboarding was banned from the resort until 1986. The US Forest Service labeled snowboards "non-directional devices".

Now that's a sinister citation.

The uninitiated must have imagined that snowboarders just tore off down the slope on "devices" that could not be steered. Visions of wild youth careening into trees, skiers, lift lines and the disco must have exploded in some bureaucrat's head.

So the sport went underground in Arizona. Or to be more precise—nocturnal. Guerilla snowboarders befriended the snocat drivers who groomed the trails at night. They got rides up the mountain, and in the glare of their headlights, boarded back down.

Now snocats are very big pieces of equipment. Sorta like the machines at the beginning of the first *Terminator* movie. They've got these scary tank treads that can squish anything in their path. Snowboarding in front of one of these monsters must have been, well, thrilling. And a real incentive to get good.

As in never, ever falling.

MAJOR POINTS

SHOP, BEG AND BORROW

Snowboarding ain't cheap. Mountains aren't free and gear is expensive. You can rent board and boots for now, but you'll have to buy suitable clothing if you can't borrow. Lift tickets, lessons (strongly recommended), travel (for most) and food all add up. In order to rent a snowboard, you'll need to lay down a bunch of cash, a credit card or your next of kin.

So it's important to shop for the closest ski area and the best deals on tickets, rentals and lessons. That means asking around. Using the yellow pages and calling here and there. Try and borrow as much gear as you can. A little planning and prep will save you major dollars. Remember, for now you just want to get into the snow. Not into debt.

LESSONS

Place yourself in the hands of a real live instructor when you first go up. Good or bad, it's still a better place to start than by yourself. You may ask, "Then why the book?" Because you'll forget and/or the lesson won't cover stuff very well or at least well enough for you at the time. Instructors are people dealing with time constraints (and kook after kook like you.) Details are lost in the translation. This book has all the basics down for reference — it is intended to complement your lessons with a living breathing expert.

TIME

Allow for all the snafus. They will occur. Your first days on the slopes will be very long and tiring. Don't add to the frustrations of learning by running late for lessons. Leave early for the mountains. Don't believe 'em when they say the drive is only 2 hours. Give yourself 3 . Believe me — it'll take time to find the place, park, buy tickets, rent gear and put it all on. You'll be amazed at how long it takes to lace your boots with freezing fingers.

FITNESS

The kinda shape you're in will be evident in 45 minutes, once you've staggered onto the slopes. If you're in lousy shape, you'll die. If you're in O.K. shape, you'll die. If you're in good shape, you'll be exhausted.

Don't be stupid. Be in shape. This snowboarding stuff is a lotta work at first. And get a good night's sleep the night before.

DESIRE

Make no bones about it. Snowboarding is a challenging sport to learn. You'll need patience, practice, and concentration. But above all, you'll need desire. You gotta want it.

TRUE GRIT

There was once a very determined young man who was seriously bitten by the snowboarding bug. However, he had a problem. No car. And he lived a long, long way from the snow.

It took some doing, but he managed to turn on a friend of his (who had wheels) to the thrill and glory of his new found sport. Soon thereafter they headed out to the mountains. Unfortunately, the driver did not have a good day. Without instruction and little help from his friend, he pretty much ate snow all morning. After about three hours of that slamming sensation, he'd had enough. He was goin' home.

But the hero of our story was having none of that. He'd stay, by golly, shred all day and worry about getting home later! So he stayed and his ride left.

The ski area closed at 4:30. Our guy stuck out his thumb and began what turned out to be his own little Battan Death March. Now all this happened in early February '93 in Southern California. The time is important because that is when the biggest storms in ten years rattled through our state. It was a National Disaster. Literally. As in flooding, torrential rains, mud slides, and lots and lots and lots of snow.

Anyway, this manly man hitchhiked over 200 miles through the howling weather because he wanted to snowboard a full day's worth. It took him twelve hours. He got home at 4:00 a.m. the next day.

There are all kinds of things we have to be dedicated to: making enough money, brushing your teeth, obeying traffic signs, changing the oil filter, etc. . . . But it sure is nice to be dedicated to something that frees the spirit and is actually FUN! Although this particular episode is a tad extreme, it does illustrate an important point or two about achieving a goal. You gotta want it and sometimes you gotta sacrifice. Snowboarding is well worth the effort. Give it all you got!

GEAR

WARM AND DRY

Yes, it's cold up there. And wet. Here's a handy checklist for clothing from head to toe:

- ☐ *A cap or sock to cover dome and ears.*
  If it's real cold, you'll want a mask.

- ☐ *Sunglasses or goggles that will fit over your glasses.*
  Without them, the sun's glare off the snow will drill your sockets.

- ☐ *Layers of loose-fitting torso garb.*
  Start with a t-shirt, then sweatshirt or sweaters. Top it off with a waterproof jacket or pullover. Dressing in layers allows you to add or subtract clothing in increments.

Dressed and Equipped — Robin wears a knit cap, sun goggles, waterproof jacket, waterproof pants and soft snowboarding boots. Underneath it all he's 'layered' in t-shirt(s), sweatshirt(s), and sweatpants. Note the waterproof gloves and the loose fit of the clothing.

The snowboard is a freestyle model. Note the symmetrical shape and the identical nose/tail design. This type of board is relatively easy to maneuver and excellent to learn on.

Snowboard Profile — The board is 'twin-tipped,' enabling the rider to ride backwards. (Not that you will soon!) Note the highback bindings which are the usual bindings of choice for freestyle riding. The safety strap will attach to Robin's front leg.

- □ *Gloves.*
  These should definitely be waterproof. No knits.
- □ *Loose fitting sweats under waterproof pants.*
  Ski pants are fine. It's very important that your trousers be waterproof because you're gonna be on your butt a lot.

- □ *A healthy pair of athletic socks.*

SUNSCREEN

Your face will fry without it! Protect your skin and prevent skin cancer.

BOOTS AND BOARD

The Ideal

If you can, rent boots and board from somebody in your home town the day before you go up.* This may be the least expensive way to rent and it gives you the time to comfortably acquaint yourself with board, boots, laces, straps, buckles, etc. Much better to learn how to don all this new gear with a friendly sales person in a cozy showroom than in a freezing parking lot. Or a crowded rental room at a ski area with a clerk who's too busy to care.

Renting from a local shop will give you the time to make all the adjustments you might need on your bindings and to ask 1,001 neophyte questions like, "How do you stop one of these things?" Your local shop will become your first and major source for gear, information and fellowship anyway. Might as well start there.

---

*If you can, take gear home and do the carpet test. Clear a space on your rug and put everything on. Practice buckling and unbuckling, walking, and turning around (see Chapter 5). With both feet strapped in, lean up on your toes and back on your heels. This will give you a feel for things before you hit the slopes.

Soft Snow - boarding Boot(s) — Each boot has an inner and outer boot that laces.

No Local Shop?

There should be shops surrounding the ski area you intend to visit. Check them out. And call the ski areas. This could be your best bet. You might be able to get a package deal for everything at one place — lift tickets, gear and lessons. Then you won't have to hassle driving back and forth between places. Anything that can make arrangements simpler and cheaper is the optimum route your first day out.

Special Note

Renting a snowboard entails a deposit of about $400. Or a credit card. They should tell you that on the phone. Prepare yourself.

Boots

Soft snowboarding boots are really boots, unlike the Frankenstein shoes skiers must wear. They are

29
940491

Properly Adjusted Bindings — The rear binding is at right angles to the board. The front binding is angled slightly forward, like Robin's foot.

Buckling Up — Good and snug, but not tight. Secure your ankle first, then your toes.

comfortable and easy to walk around in. Each boot has an inner and outer boot that laces. They are heavily padded and have thick rubber soles. Like ultra duck boots.

In order to wear soft boots, your snowboard must have highback bindings. The board you should be learning on, an all-purpose/freestyle model, will have them.

Make sure the padding isn't ripped. Make sure all the laces are there. And most important — make sure they fit snug, without your toes hitting the end. Loose boots will wreck your ankles.

Now you can wear ski boots if you have plate bindings. But. Plate bindings are usually found on alpine or racing model snowboards which are more difficult to learn on than all-purpose/freestyle boards. So. If you're a skier and prefer to learn in ski boots, it's wise to find an all-purpose/freestyle snowboard with plate bindings. This, however, may not be easy to do.

Board

Rent an all-purpose/freestyle board. Stay away from the alpine or racing models. All-purpose/freestyle boards are 'looser' and easier to maneuver than the alpine or racing boards, which are much 'stiffer'.

Check out the bindings. The front bindings should angle a tad towards the front of the board. The rear bindings should be at right angles to the board. Both should be screwed down tight.

Strap yourself in and see how it feels. You'll have a natural inclination to put one or the other foot forward in a snowboarder's stance. Right foot forward is called 'goofy foot' for no real reason, and the left foot forward is called 'regular foot' for no real reason. Just do what feels right for you. Once strapped in, you may want your front foot angled out more, but don't do it. Board control works by rocking from heel to toe and toe to heel at right angles to the board's length. That's how you lift your edges and turn. You can't do that with your feet turned out.

Fiddle with the straps and buckles, if you're using highback bindings, and make sure you understand how they work. In order to use the lifts, you'll be taking your back foot out of its binding in order to walk around and glide. In a day of snowboarding, that will add up to a lot of in and out, so get good at buckling and unbuckling. Seriously.

If you're wearing hard-shell boots and using plate bindings, you have the advantage of being able to 'snap' in and out of your bindings. The way skiers do. The bindings only have to be adjusted once. Before you set out.

Make sure your board has a leash or safety strap. This attaches to your front leg and prevents a runaway board. A loose snowboard hurtling down the slope is a death missile. You won't get on the lifts without it.

WASTING MONEY, LOSING FACE

Talk about learning the hard way. The first two times that I went snowboarding I forgot my goggles and nearly went blind from the glare. I didn't use sunscreen either. For three days after each trip I looked like I did a head dip into a pail of cranberry juice. I also got ripped for fifty bucks on a lift-lesson-rental package because I didn't shop the ski area twenty minutes down the road. It's easy for bad things to happen if you're unprepared.

Check into things. Have a plan. Know what you're doing. I hate to plan stuff so I can understand what a drag this may sound like. But I'm telling you . . . poor planning can really cut into the fun and fun is what this is all about. So get prepped the best way possible in order to have a good time . . . even on your first day.

FINAL PREPARATIONS

FINAL CHECK

Before you begin your journey to the mountains, consider a number of things. (Oh, no.) Yes. Another checklist.

- ☐ *Call ahead for conditions.*
  Make sure the roads are clear. You may need chains or snow tires. Better ask. Make sure the snow has a good foundation. You can't learn on ice or very well in slush.

- ☐ *Bring extra clothing.*
  You'll probably need to change after you've wiped out 32 times.

- ☐ *Bring your own food and plenty of liquids.*
  Unless you don't mind $5 hot dogs or $2 sodas.

- ☐ *Make sure you know where you're going.*
  Bring a map.

- ☐ *Money and credit cards.*
  For rentals, emergencies, incidentals, and bribes.

- ☐ *All your gear.*

- ☐ *A tank full of gas.*

- ☐ *Desire.*

YOU MADE IT

At last. For most of us it takes a while to get to a ski area. But it's well worth it. The air is crisp, clean, and clear. After a fresh snow it's like being in a postcard. Sweeping, snow-covered slopes, towering peaks, and a billion trees . . . Half the reason for doing this is just being there.

A sport that blends the power and beauty of nature is something to treasure. Snowboarding is being a PART of all that splendor. It's about being a PAR-TICIPANT. It'll take some time to really feel yourself get in tune with your board and the mountain, but you'll get it soon enough. And the returns will well be worth the investment!

DOWN TO BUSINESS

Now it's time to play window bingo. Buy your lift tickets here, your lesson ticket there, and your rentals (if you haven't rented somewhere else) down the stairs and around to your left, behind the restaurant. Some ski areas may be more convenient than others, but make sure you have given yourself plenty of time to get lost.

When you buy your lift ticket, make sure you get the wire hooking device that attaches the ticket to you. They'll be hanging in bunches next to the window. The ticket is printed on sticky back. Peel off the backing and fold it over the fat end of the wire AFTER you hook the wire through the loop of something you're wearing. Your ticket needs to be plainly seen in order to use the lifts.

Find the rental shop and get fitted for boots and board. Make sure the boots aren't too mangled and that all the laces are intact. Make sure the fit is snug without your toes banging against the toe of the boot.

Check out the board. Make sure the bindings are all there and that you understand how to use them. Make sure you have a leash. Keep your eye on the clock! Don't be late for your class. Find the place to buy your lesson ticket.

Stash your street shoes in a locker or in your car, and put on your boots. Lace 'em up snug. On to your lesson.

(The next two chapters deal with fundamental snowboarding technique. Your lesson should cover this stuff, more or less.)

BUT THIS TIME I'M NOT FOOLIN'!

Treks on and off the mountains can be tricky no matter how well you plan. My pal Stu, for example, still has his neck hairs standing on end over this incident.

First of all, you gotta understand Stu. Stu is the kind of guy who will call you up impersonating the IRS. Hardy har har har. Big joker. Draws things on your car window. Throws wax and kelp at you when you're trying to catch a wave. Leaves banana peels on your windshield. Get the picture?

Anyway, Stu's driving his truck back down the mountain after a long day of snowboarding. He's got six guys piled in the back. It's freezing. And all of a sudden Stu shouts, "I DON'T HAVE ANY BRAKES!"

Nobody believes him of course. After all, he's the cut-up, right? But, hey, nice try, Stu.

So picture this. It's dark, cold, and the truck is careening down the steepest grade of the peak . . . going faster and faster. Stu is going nuts because there REALLY AREN'T ANY BRAKES, and he's starting to think that EVERYBODY IS GOING TO DIE.

And no one believes him.

But the man does prevail. He gently coaxes the runaway truck to a halt, using the emergency brake. Which had to be a chore, because he's got one of these really big trucks. By now, everybody is a believer after watching Stu grunt and groan with the hand brake. Everybody wipes the cold sweat from their brows. (Thank you, Lord.)

Seems the brake calipers actually froze up, rendering the foot brake useless. Luckily, the emergency brake didn't suffer the same fate. After dousing the drums with water, the calipers un-stuck, and the journey home resumed.

This ditty illustrates the need to respect the mountains in winter time. The weather is a force to be reckoned with, indeed. BE AWARE!

WALKIN, GLIDIN, SLIDIN

Find yourself a gently sloping area at the base of your mountain with flat areas above and below. Make sure you're off to the side and away from skiers and other snowboarders.

PUTTING THE BOARD ON

Once you have arrived at your level area, set your board down and strap your front foot into the forward binding. Again, that's the foot you've already discovered to be your natural choice to lead the way. Secure your ankle first, then your toes. The bindings should be good and snug. Strap the leash up and around your leg, below the knee. There should be no slack.

WALKING

The weirdness begins. With your front foot cramped into this impossible pigeon toe, slide the board forward and straight ahead. Take steps with your free

Leash or Safety Strap — Attaches to the front leg, below the knee.

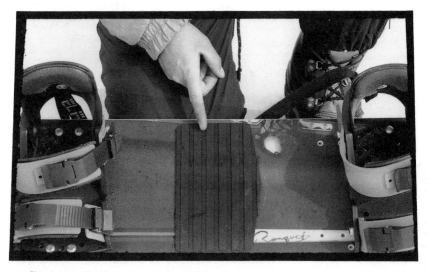

Stomp Pad — A rubber-like patch to rest your unbound foot while gliding.

foot alongside the board. Try and keep it all pointed straight ahead. Keep your steps small so that your legs won't splay apart. This is awkward, I know. The board will want to veer out on its merry way. But this you must get down. This is how you'll negotiate lift lines.

Practice walking for a bit, then stop and turn yourself around, lifting and turning the boarded foot in small increments. Maneuver your free foot next to the board in order to prevent it from running away. Now go the other way. No, this is not fun.

GLIDING

Try a glide. Digging your free foot into the snow, build up some speed as if you were on a skateboard. Again, keep your free foot close to the board, and take small steps. When you have enough speed to glide, place your free foot on the stomp pad located between the two bindings. Balance yourself over the center of the board, with knees slightly bent, torso turned a bit forward, and bent at the waist. Use your arms as balancing beams and look straight ahead. Look at the other snowboarders and see how they stand. It's like riding a bike. Once you feel it — you got it.

All this is new and absolutely cumbersome. All the more reason you should practice these things a bit before you do anything else.

WALKING UP A HILL

You advance up a hill with your free foot in the lead, and your boarded foot at right angles to the slope. Position the board sideways to the slope, and dig the uphill edge into the snow. Push off the anchored board and take a small step up the hill with your free foot. Lift the board, keeping it at right angles to the slope, and bring it alongside your free foot. This will get you up a little hill.

Walking—Note the ridiculous angle of the front foot. This will drive you nuts at first. The trick is to keep your board and free foot close together and to take small steps. This will help prevent splaying. Slide the board straight ahead in small increments and step up with your free foot. Slide and step. Slide and step. More pix next page.

Turning Around — Pivot around your free foot, lifting and landing the board around in small increments. Try and keep foot and board close together to avoid the wishbone effect.

Gliding — Push with your free foot and keep the board pointed straight ahead.

Once you've gained some speed, rest your free foot on the stomp pad located between the bindings. This picture also illustrates how you'll glide off the lifts.

SLIDING STRAIGHT DOWN

Once you've made it up the slope onto level snow, strap the other foot onto the board. You may have to kneel or sit down to accomplish this at first. Get your balance while standing still. Get a feel for the stance. It should feel much better than the glide stance since your feet are strapped wider apart.

Sort of hop yourself from the level area to the beginning of the downhill slope. If you're too far away from the slope, you'll have to unstrap your rear foot and walk closer. Once the board begins to move, just let it go where it wants. LOOK AHEAD where you're going, and NOT AT THE BOARD. Settle into the stance you had when you practiced gliding. Slide straight down until you stop.

A WORD ABOUT STOPPING

It isn't like skiing. You don't ever just neatly stop and relax on your feet, on the slopes. The board wants to move. Since you're strapped in, and strapped in on one thing instead of two separate things, maintaining your balance while being still is pretty much impossible. So, if you really want to stop and stay put on the slopes, sit on your can.

As you learn more about edge control your ability to stop will improve dramatically. We'll get into that in the next chapter. Right now you should be sliding on an eeny little hill at the base of which you can more or less glide to a halt.

You can slow down and stop (sort of) after you slide by rocking back on your heels or up on your toes and digging your UPHILL EDGE. Then you'll flap your arms wildly and fall down. Since stopping is 'iffy' at this point, it's a real good idea to stay away from everybody and everything in the beginning.

Before you buckle up, make sure the bindings are free of snow.

Strapping In — It's easy to do sitting down. Strap ankles first, then your toes.

Hopping — You can travel short distances once you're strapped in by jumping. Yes, these 'hops' are a bit exaggerated.

46

The Stance — After walking and gliding this will feel great! Face forward, look up and out with knees slightly bent and arms spread for balance.

Stopping Backside —
Rock back on your heels
and dig the uphill edge
of your snowboard.

Stopping Frontside —
Rock forward on your
toes and dig the uphill
edge.

48

FALLING DOWN

This you'll get good at. And that's O.K. Everybody wipes out. You just don't want to get hurt, of course. Stay away from the difficult runs until you know how to deal with them. And try to avoid catching your downhill edge. Edges are the sides of the snowboard. Catching your downhill edge means that you will fall downhill, hard and fast. Uphill falls are much easier to take. The distance is shorter to fall and recovering from them is much simpler.

Up to now, you've been going straight down a bunny slope and edges have not been involved. If you fall, it's because you lost your balance and the falls should be relatively mild. Just make sure your hands are balled up in loose fists in order to avoid jammed fingers.

As you progress up the slopes and try new things you'll self-destruct in any number of unique and interesting ways. In this chapter I've inserted eight full pages of photos illustrating various recovery techniques.

Don't let the wipeouts get you down! It is a part of the process. Take one thing at a time. Without time-tables, pressures, or expectations.

EASY DOES IT

A special word about the dynamics of our sport. Gravity pulls you down lickety split on a snowy slope if you're attached to a snowboard. The steeper the hill, the faster you go. And boy, it's a lot faster than you think if you've never tried it. And that's what makes this sport so much fun. Flying down the face of a mountain is one of those living-in-the-moment experiences we sometimes have (and should have a heck of a lot more of).

But. When you first try the sport, you cannot deal with much steepness without serious consequences.

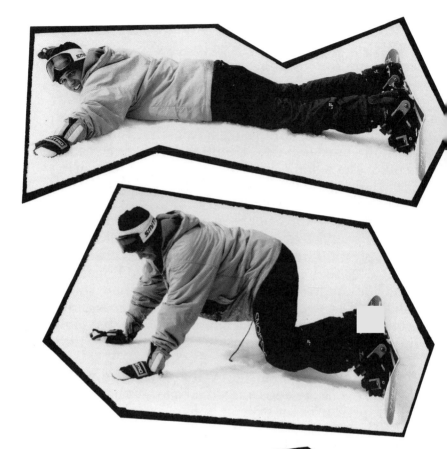

To get up from an **uphill faceplant**, dig the uphill edge of your board and scoot back. Keep the board sideways to the slope.

50

Getting up from an **uphill buttplant** is a snap. Just keep the board sideways to the slope and rock forward. Use your hands as balance points. More pix next page.

51

These don't feel good. If you have fallen downhill, it's because you caught your downhill edge. Getting up from a **downhill faceplant** isn't too difficult. Again, keep your board at right angles to the slope until you're ready to slide. More pix next page.

Skygazing from a **downhill buttplant**. This takes some doing. First lift and dig the tail of your board into the snow. Then roll over and scoot up. Keep the board sideways, of course. More pix next page.

Without practice and training, sliding down even an intermediate slope is like running across the freeway.

If you're good at surfing or hang gliding or tennis or racquetball or any sport (I mean good), you have the tendency to approach new sports with a tad too much confidence. Sublime idiots among us have refined this into a cult of machoism. "I am a man. I will be a man. I will take that hill. And be manly about it", etc., etc. Yes, this actually goes on in many, many minds.*

Let me tell you about my first 45 minutes on a snowboard. I slammed into the mountain about six times. Twice on my back, twice on my face, twice in some other way I don't want to talk about. I cracked a rib. I got whiplash. I knocked the wind out of myself every time. And I mean the real thing. The pain was one thing, but what was worse was the fatigue. All that pounding just sapped me. I never fully recovered that day. I just can't remember ever . . . being . . . so . . . trashed.

Too much speed plus too little training equals mishap. Every snowboarder I know has a first-day story about horrific falls, etc. Like it's part of the plan or something. But let me tell you this. I wish I'da been a bunny man that day and gotten qualified instruction. I would have snowboarded longer and learned more. I wouldn't have gotten so beat and tired.

Take it easy your first day. Take lessons. Work on the basics in a forgiving environment with a forgiving attitude toward yourself. I honestly think you can learn this sport without killing yourself first. This is a revolutionary concept in some circles (and inflammatory among real men), but hey . . . why don't you prove me right.

---

*O.K., O.K. Women can be just as headstrong and cocky. And that's what I mean by 'manly'. I'm referring then to both 'manly' men AND 'manly' women. (What?)

NOTES

6

DOIN' IT!

EDGES! EDGES! EDGES!

Flying straight down the hill is thrilling, sure. But in order to have any kind of control over the snowboard, you must learn how to turn and traverse both ways. Turning is how you change direction. Traversing is how you slide sideways across the trail. You must be a competent turner and traverser before you can negotiate steeper runs with any real confidence. Otherwise, you'll just barrel along until you run into something or panic and fall.

Whenever you turn or traverse on a slope, edges control your movement. As mentioned before, edges refer to the sides of your snowboard. EXCEPT WHEN YOU FLY STRAIGHT DOWN OR DURING THE NANO-SECOND YOU TRANSFER EDGES DURING A TURN, NEVER RIDE FLAT FOOTED ON THE FLAT OF YOUR BOARD. All other maneuvers

Riding the Uphill Edge — When you angle or traverse across the slope, you always ride the uphill edge. Either on your toes or on your heels.

(short of acrobatics) require that you RIDE THE UPHILL EDGE ON YOUR TOES (frontside) OR ON YOUR HEELS (backside). The uphill edge is the side of the snowboard facing uphill. The downhill edge faces downhill. There are only two edges. YOU CANNOT RIDE YOUR DOWNHILL EDGE. As soon as it touches snow it will catch and slam you down.

This chapter concerns edges and working in concert with them. This is what downhill snowboarding is all about. There will be three parts or steps:

1. Skidding — This is riding the board sideways down the hill. It's a good place to start because THIS IS HOW YOU STOP! It'll also familiarize you with that all-important uphill edge.
2. Traversing — This is angling this way and that down the slope. It's how you control your descent. Yep. On your uphill edge.
3. Turning — And this is where all this business is headed. Transferring edges and changing direction.

UP THE MOUNTAIN

In order to learn about edges it's necessary to practice on a steeper slope. You need a little speed to acquaint yourself properly with skidding, traversing and turning. The bunny slopes are great for learning basic sliding technique, but they just don't provide the gravitational pull you'll need to feel the edges of your snowboard work.

Find an intermediate trail. Usually such trails are marked by a blue square. As opposed to a green dot (beginner) or a black diamond (expert). What you want is a hill with enough steepness to get you going but not so much as to ignite any vertigo. Don't worry. The first thing you're going to learn is how to apply the brakes.

That is, after you negotiate the lifts. . . .

Getting On the Lift — Position yourself well ahead of the advancing chair.

As you get scooped up, make sure you lift the nose of your board!

Getting Off the Lift — As you settle down, scoot up onto the edge of the chair, point the board straight ahead, and lean forward in a crouch.

63

USING THE LIFTS

When using the lifts, be alert, ready and attentive to the attendants. And you should do fine.

Getting On

Using the glide walk, join the lift line at the end. It's polite not to stomp on others' equipment. As soon as the chair before yours swoops by, scoot up to the loading area and look behind you. Make sure your butt is aimed toward the middle of the advancing chair. As you get scooped up, grab ahold of the chair.

Face forward and LIFT THE NOSE OF YOUR SNOWBOARD. If your board digs into the snow here, you will either dismount hard and fast or leave a leg. Settle your weight in a balanced way on the seat. Now is a good time to kick off any snow stuck on your board. Resting the board on your free foot helps to ease its dangling weight. Enjoy the view! Watch the boarders below. This is a great place to study others' technique. And curb the desire to jump off.

Getting Off

Truly one of the more humbling experiences in all of sports. It takes a time or two to gain control, so take a chair by yourself if possible. As your chair dips down into the unloading area, POINT YOUR BOARD STRAIGHT AHEAD with the tip up. Position your free foot on the stomp pad. You should be sitting forward. As your board hits the snow, lean forward, stand up in a slight crouch and concentrate on your balance.

The momentum of the lift should be just enough to gently shove you down the slight incline. Just glide to a halt. If you fall, get up immediately and walk out of the unloading zone.

I CAN'T GO DOWN THAT!

O.K. You're on top of an intermediate hill. If it's your first time, you'll be amazed at how steep it is (my God!), but you will get over that. You just need to build your confidence. And in order to do that, you need to know how to control the stick strapped to your feet.

PART ONE: SKIDDING

Walk over to the incline that leads to the slope. Remember to keep yourself to the side of the trail. Strap your other foot in. Make sure boots and binding are secure and snug. Facing down the hill, place the board at right angles to the slope of the trail. That is, sideways. Now stand and let yourself slide down sideways. Rock back on your heels in order to prevent your downhill edge from catching. Just let yourself go where the board wants. Balance yourself evenly on the heels of both feet, with knees slightly bent. Keep the board sideways by shifting your weight ever so slightly here and there.

You will move at a slow pace, because the board is not pointed down the slope. You can control your speed by rocking on your heels. Rock back to slow, stall or stop. Roll forward to gain speed. But never lay the board flat on the snow. It will immediately dig its downhill edge and spill you down the hill. RIDE THE UPHILL EDGE. If you need to stop, rock back, slow down and simply sit.

Skidding is how you shall deal with all your troubles on the slopes, especially in the beginning. This is how you start and finish everything. This is how you can begin to confront the mountain with confidence. Because no matter where you are, you can get down the mountain in one piece. Free from fear.

Skidding Backside — Knees are slightly bent and weight is evenly distributed as you ride on your heels. The downhill edge rides above the slope's surface.

Skidding Frontside — This time on your toes. Again riding the uphill edge. Note the gap between the downhill edge and the snow.

NOW THE OTHER SIDE

The physics are the same, except you're facing uphill and you're balancing yourself on your toes. Again, never lay the board flat on the slope. The downhill edge must always clear the snow. Some people find either frontside or backside preferable. You need to feel comfortable with both because frontside AND backside positions are central to turning and traversing back and forth across the slope. You can't learn to turn just one way.

NO PROBLEM. I SKID.

My first real appreciation of the sideways skid occurred the second day I ever snowboarded.

Somehow my buddy and I got lost. We wound up a-way back thar somewhere with 15 minutes left until closing. And we were both very, very tired.

Luckily, we stumbled onto a skier who was happy to show us the way back to the parking lot. I remember staggering over to the edge of the final descent (I was walking it because for some reason, there was no elevation between lifts) and looking down at my worst nightmare.

It was absolutely vertical. A long-way-down vertical. A long-way-down vertical with all these . . . bumps. (I've since learned that these bumps are called moguls.)

Anyway, it was pretty scary. But being the men we was, we turned our boards at right angles to the sheer drop and skidded all . . . the . . . way . . . down. No, not very dashing. But healthy.

Beating the fear monster is one of the first things you gotta do as you learn. And you do that sideways. Learn how to skid.

PART TWO: TRAVERSING
(Angling Down the Hill)

When you skid down the mountain, you are following the fall line. That is, you are moving straight down the steepest part of a given slope. As soon as you begin to nose the front of your board downhill, you will slide across the fall line. This is called traversing. Angling into the fall line speeds you up, angling out or past the fall line slows you down.

To make this simple, we'll just use the parameters of the ski trail. The steepest part of the trail is the middle. Angling into the middle will be fast until you pass it and reach the other side. You can control your speed as you traverse by decreasing your downhill angle. That is, by digging your uphill edge until you begin to travel in a more and more sideways direction to the slope of the mountain. As soon as you are completely at right angles to the fall line, you will stall.

Obviously, once you've angled one way across the trail and past the fall line to the other side, you have to go the other way. Or just skid down. Hence the need to turn.

ANGLING BACKSIDE
(On Your Heels)

Make sure you have room to travel in the direction of your angle. From the standing skid position, let the nose of your snowboard find its way downhill — real gradual-like. You'll notice immediately an increase in speed. That be gravity. But don't panic. Remember, all you ever have to do to slow down is decrease that downhill angle, and resume the skid position. Also remember that backside skidding or angling means always standing on your heels. Think in terms of

Backside Traverse — From a backside skid position, drop the nose of your board and angle across the slope. More pix next page.

Ride on your heels on
the uphill edge of your
board. Stop by rocking
backwards.

This is what you do before you learn how to turn. When you've traversed as far as you can, stop and lay down with your board downhill. Dig the tail of your board into the snow and roll over.

riding the uphill edge of your board. Never the flat bottom. So riding backside means riding on your heels on the uphill edge. Never flat-footed on the flat bottom.

Angle along the face of the slope all the way to the other side. Control your speed by rocking back on your heels. Rock back to slow, roll forward to speed up. Don't let the board get ahead of you. GET YOURSELF OVER THE BOARD. Keep it under you. Slow down and stop once you've reached the other side. This will probably mean sitting on your can. Monkey yourself around in order to face the other way. (Don't bother with a turn just yet.)

Frontside Traverse — Drop the nose of your board from a frontside skid position and ride the uphill edge on your toes. Control your speed by rocking forward (slower), and backwards (faster). More pix next page.

Doin' It!

To slow down or stop, rock forward and dig the uphill edge.

NOW GO FRONTSIDE
(On Your Toes)

This time pop up on your toes in order to use that all-important uphill edge. Always on your toes, angle back across the trail. Again, control your speed by controlling the angle of your descent. Way up on your toes to slow down. Rock back to speed up. REMEMBER, AS YOU TRAVERSE YOU NEVER RIDE FLAT FOOTED OR FLAT ON THE BOTTOM OF THE BOARD. IT'S ALWAYS HEEL OR TOE IN CONCERT WITH THE UPHILL EDGE.

DON'T DO THIS, O.K.?

This is how I learned about edges.

Without a clue as to what snowboarding was all about, I took a lift up my first hill. It wasn't very steep really. I mean I look at it now and laugh. But at the time it may as well have been the Matterhorn.

My so-called "instructor" went down the hill first. He stopped at the bottom and waved me down. "Go this way and then go that way," he shouted, waving his arms this way and that way. "Let's work on your turns."

Shoving off, I went "this way" fine. Real smooth, in fact. My stance felt right and I held out my arms like a real shred-master. Man, I must have looked sharp.

Going "that way" was a problem though. My "instructor" was waving and yelling, "Turn! Turn!" But I realized I simply had no idea how to crank this sucker around. It was going hell-bent-for-leather for the trees, and for the life of me I could not locate the steering wheel.

So, I turned . . . my body. Thinking the board would surely follow.

When I opened my eyes I saw nothing but blue sky. And stars. My head was buried in a foot of snow. My lungs were collapsed and my neck was starting to swell.

"Instructor-man" boarded up to my body and asked if I was all right. I immediately answered in the affirmative although that was not the case. At all.

He announced, "This is what happens when you catch an edge. Don't catch your edge, O.K.?"

Now learning about things can happen in a lotta ways. You can stick your hand into a flame and learn about heat. You can run across the freeway and learn about car velocity. You can jump into a lion's cage and learn about teeth.

And you can learn about snowboarding the hard way, too.

It does make for some interesting stories. If you survive. But trust me on this. There is a more intelligent (huh?) way to go about it. Really.

PART THREE: TURNING

Going from one direction to another is turning. Turning is how you get down the mountain, unless you skid or pommel straight down the fall line on the flat of your snowboard. The latter is not recommended. And skidding you'll get tired of. Real fast.

This is where it gets hard. Hard as in losing control and falling down. You'll probably spend most of your first day (or two) trying to do this. You will get frustrated. But don't give up! It's a matter of timing and feel. You'll get it. It's sorta like learning how to drive a stick shift. Remember how impossible it was to coordinate speed, clutch, and gear shifting?

The dynamics of going down a mountain are fairly simple. Turning into the fall line speeds you up, passing it slows you down. For now, you will learn to turn as you pass the fall line.

Starting with a backside traverse, make your journey from one side of the trail to the other. As you near the far side, you should be slowing down, as you have passed the fall line. Weight should be on your front foot. Nose your board downhill. Yes, for a nanosecond you will use the flat of your feet and board and for that nanosecond, the board will say to you, "MY EDGE HAS BEEN RELEASED! TURN ME OR DIE!" Listen to your board. Rock yourself to your toes and push the tail around with your back foot.

This is transferring your edges or turning. What was once your uphill edge is now the dreaded downhill edge and must never touch the snow until you've reached the other side of the trail. There, of course, you will slow down, nose the board downhill with weight forward until you feel it whisper to you again. Then you'll rock to your heels in order to change edges. Again pushing the board around with your rear foot.

Sounds simple enough. But it won't be. Because for now you're thinking the board is one (strange) thing and you another.

But then you'll crank that first turn.

When you finally feel the edges transfer responsibilities underneath you, and you smoothly swoop around without crashing, it'll make all the butt- and headplants a distant memory.

You see, turning is the essence of this sport. It's what transforms you from an awkward survivor to a PARTICIPANT. Check out the riders who really rip. Look at the effortless manner in which they change direction. No matter what speed. It's because they know how to work their edges and TURN. And you'll get it. Sure you'll eat it, but once you get the feel for turning both ways, it'll be a brand new world. All of a sudden steepness, snow and speed will become very, very cool things.

Backside or Heel Turn — From a frontside traverse, put your weight forward, drop the nose of your board downhill, rock back on your heels and push the board around with your rear foot. More pix next page.

As you come out of the turn into a backside traverse, you'll be riding on your heels.

Frontside or Toe Turn — From a backside traverse, put your weight forward, drop the nose downhill, rock onto your toes and push around with your back leg.

The edges have been transferred. The turn is complete. You are now traversing frontside and riding the uphill edge on your toes.

THAT'S ALL?

Hardly. Like I said, this is just a primer to get you going. To familiarize you with the edges of your snowboard and hopefully to get you turning, which is usually the major hump for beginners.

The art of turning is an ongoing thing and something you'll get better at as you practice, practice, practice. Someone else will have to teach you those impossible maneuvers you see in the magazines and on the video.

So keep at it. Watch the snowboarders who came before you and keep learning. One day, you'll find you can snowboard all day without feeling sore the next morning. But more importantly, you'll be able to capture for yourself the secrets of flying down a mountain in complete control. HAVE FUN!

SWEETSPOT

I'd been snowboarding a lot before I made this one turn. It's not that I hadn't made a hundred before this one. It's just that this one really felt like, well . . . how I imagined a great turn should feel.

I was at Squaw Valley, California. Truly the queen of the Sierras. Vast, swooping slopes. A gigantic bowl that lets you rip at will. I suppose that had something to do with it.

Anyway. I was straightening out on this one run. I let my speed build until the trail began to dog leg. Then I rose on my toes and banked a turn. No skidding. No overturning. Just a perfect cranking turn that seemed to last twice as long as any I had ever had.*

---

*I found out later that what I had done was a "carve". Most snowboards have concave edges called sidecuts, the radius of which makes a circle. The turn followed the true round of my board without me skidding the back end around with my leg. The physics of it all are somewhat vague in my mind, but the feeling was wonderful!

Connecting Turns —
From a frontside tra-
verse, Robin heel turns
into a backside tra-
verse . . .

Doin' It!

. . . toe turns into a
frontside traverse . . .

. . . and heel turns into a backside traverse. Note Robin's form and the edges of his snowboard as he progresses through this sequence.

A turn like that is impossible to describe in words. Every sport has its sweetspots and I guess that was my first with snowboarding. Turning is a basic function of downhill travel, but can be a higher form of art when mind, body and mountain meet in concert on the edge of a snowboard.

SAFETY

Folks who know a lot more than I put this together:

SNOWBOARDER'S RESPONSIBILITY CODE: *There are elements of risk in snowboarding that common sense and personal awareness can help reduce.*

1. Snowboard under control and in such a manner that you can stop or avoid other snowboarders/skiers or objects

2. When snowboarding downhill or overtaking another snowboarder/skier, you must avoid the snowboarder/skier below you.

3. You must not stop where you obstruct a trail or are not visible to other snowboarders/skiers.

4. When entering a trail or starting downhill, yield to other snowboarders/skiers.

5. You shall use a device to prevent a runaway snowboard.

6. You shall keep off closed trails or posted areas and observe all posted signs.

Is it obvious? Skiers and snowboarders follow the same rules.

KNOW WHO YOU ARE

You're a beginner. You know nothing. You can't do anything. You're a clumsy, gasping idiot on a slat. Stay away from everybody, for God's sake!

WHEN YOU'RE TIRED, STOP

. . . and rest. You'll probably exhaust yourself sooner than you think. Especially your first day. Everything is new, awkward and difficult. You can't concentrate when you're fatigued. You can't really do anything, so take a break. For as long as it takes.

BE AWARE. ALL THE TIME

Where are you on the hill? Where is everyone else? Where are you going?

BE IN SHAPE

Hopefully, you are into something on a regular basis that requires a little muscle, a little movement, some lung power and flexibility. If you're in tune with your body, your reactions are quicker. If your body is in tune, you can take the new strains and bruises in stride. You'll have better concentration and you'll last longer.

Stretching before you start is always a good idea. You're gonna use muscles you thought you never had.

Look Up! This should not be your view as you slide.

That's Better — In order to anticipate you must be aware of the terrain ahead.

TAKE LESSONS

If you wing it alone or with a "friend who knows how," you're at risk. By yourself you'll destroy yourself. With a "friend who knows how," you'll simply have a captive (maybe) audience.

BE PATIENT

It's especially difficult to accept your clumsiness if you're actually good at other sports. It's natural, yet unrealistic, to assume that you can immediately transfer your talents to another athletic endeavor. You won't be shredding on a snowboard on your first day, so don't try. Poke around with the fundamentals on little pokey hills. There will be plenty of time for glory later.

LOOK AHEAD

One of the easiest bad habits to get into is looking down at your board. It's pretty natural to gaze down at the vehicle that you think could break your neck, but don't. You won't hurt yourself if you learn on the gentle slopes. But you could run into a tree if you don't look up. Snowboarding is a sport of lickety-split anticipation and reaction. You can't do it without concentrating on the road ahead. Learn this right away.

GOOD EQUIPMENT/GOOD FIT

Boots must fit good and snug without toes hitting the end. All the laces must be there, and the boots must provide firm support. Exactly the same with bindings. Check for loose screws, buckles, etc.

SUNSCREEN

You have not been burnt until you've been burned on the snow.

SUNGLASSES OR SUN GOGGLES

Without them, you will go blind. And headaches you won't believe.

FALLING DOWN

This is a tough one, because the worst falls cannot be anticipated. When you catch an edge, you'll slam down before you know it. Catching an edge refers to the downhill edge of your snowboard catching and digging into the snow. What you can do is work on keeping yourself loose as you run through these various exercises. Tumbles will be less of a shock if muscles aren't tense. Tense muscles will cramp your style anyway.

FEAR

It's not natural to slip and slide. It's an uncommon feeling, and can be frightening. If you're learning on the proper terrain, you won't get hurt if you fall. Stay on the gentler slopes, work on your lessons and don't be afraid.

Fear is so weird. It'll make you anticipate mishap after mishap until that's all you'll have. Learn where you're comfy and have faith in your instructor and yourself.

WHEN IN DOUBT — USE YOUR HEAD.

BONKING

This is the funniest word in the book. Or most anywhere for that matter.

Bonking is intentionally ramming into things on your snowboard. Some snowboarders will bonk anything. Trees, cars, rails, houses, boulders . . . You name it.

And it's catchy. I saw this little boy on skis one day. He was about two feet tall. He got off the lift and instead of skiing towards the open trail with his parents, he headed straight for a little tree, so he could bonk off of it. His mom and dad were beside themselves. But hey. You could tell little Johnny had seen those snowboarding hoodlums at play and wanted to hit something real bad hisself.

Bonking is not encouraged for beginner snowboarders (or skiers). None of the various acrobatics, airborne or otherwise, are. It's enough to learn about edge control for now. And very important to do so first.

Many novice snowboarders just can't wait to try the stuff they see the experts do. That's not cool because beginners have not developed any real control over their boards. They usually prove to be a danger to themselves and others. Just ask those folks hanging around the lodge with those nifty looking knee braces.

LEARN THE BASICS FIRST. MASTER YOUR EDGES!

You've got plenty of time to bonk, or leap, or spin, or flip or twirl later.

COURTESY

$\mathbf{S}$nowboarders courteous? The terms aren't necessarily contradictory. Although there has been concern that they just might be. Being a snowboarder only means you slide in the snow on one slat, not two. It doesn't mean you have to be a lout. Or that you should expect a snowboarder to be one. There is no physical reason why snowboarders and skiers cannot share the slopes. So it comes down to the golden rule: TREAT OTHERS AS YOU WOULD HAVE THEM TREAT YOU.

BE AWARE OF OTHERS

The mountain doesn't belong to anybody. There isn't any localism here. Everybody had to shell out for lift tickets. So be decent to each other, and watch where you're going. All the time.

▶ Leave a comfort zone around the folks you board by. Especially beginners and children.

The middle of the trail is no place to park.

- If you run into someone or cause someone to fall, lend assistance. (You are legally responsible to do so.)

- Stay away from areas you should stay away from, such as ski classes and race courses.

- After falling, get up promptly. Don't become an obstacle.

- Go to the end of the lift line. Don't cut or bully your way. Stay off of other folks' skis or snowboard.

- Be careful when you lug your board in crowded areas.

- Move out of lift unloading areas immediately.

- Don't horse around on the lifts.

- No hanging out in the middle of the trail.

RESPECT

This is a remarkable word and easily one of the better concepts around.

- ▶ Treat your new sport with respect. It's demanding, especially at first. So concentrate on learning with a clear head, a well-rested body and a good attitude.

- ▶ Treat the mountain with respect. Don't litter. Respect flags and trail markers put up by the area, its ski school and patrol.

- ▶ Treat skiers with respect. They bought lift tickets too. And they came first. A real long time ago. If it wasn't for skiing, there wouldn't be snowboarding. At least the way we know it.

- ▶ Treat your fellow snowboarders with respect. Don't let competitive juices turn into clashes.

- ▶ Treat yourself with respect. I know it's hard in the beginning, since you're such a geek, but hey, we've all been there.

Mountains are too darn big to justify getting nasty on. Lift lines can be a drag, but at least they move. (Just think about your last commute.) There's plenty of room to roam, and hence plenty of room to be nice. Or at least civil.

WHO ME?

The image of snowboarding and snowboarders does not immediately bring to mind courteous behavior. That does not mean it isn't there, however. It's just sorta shrouded depending on the individual snowboarder.

My wife and I were preparing to spend a day skiing (her) and snowboarding (me) at Heavenly Valley, a terrific (and huge!) ski area located in South Lake

Tahoe, California. Kathleen needed to rent equipment so we stopped at a local rental shop for skis, boots and poles.

A strapping young man outfitted in snowboarder fashion (raggedy, baggy and unkempt) proceeded to wait on her. She hadn't skied in seven years so she needed plenty of help with everything. On the face of it, it looked like there might be a poor mix here. Arrogant shredder-man versus unknowing tourist-woman (and man).

My trepidation melted as our guy outfitted Kathleen. Although he never cracked a smile, his patience and professionalism was obvious as he answered every question succinctly and imparted advice freely and directly. He was helpful in other words. A delightful surprise coming from someone who at first glance looked like a caveman with a baseball cap.

As he rung us up I thanked him for the excellent service. (Something I rarely do since I rarely get it.) Kathleen chimed in as well and gave him a big, bright smile.

Well this just about did him in. His eyes got big and for a moment he was at a complete loss. You could tell he was struggling with something. The mean little man in his mind was whispering, "Kind to tourists? No way!" Yet another voice was saying, "That's a compliment, Michael. What do you say?" He was caught in the act and caught between his angels. Uh-oh.

Finally, Michael sort of shrugged, puffed out his chest, looked out the window and replied, "Yeah . . . you just got me on a good day." He finished ringing up the sale and was probably relieved that none of his buddies were around to witness all this.

My, oh, my. The thin shells of arrogance and image we all wear from time to time. Cumbersome, aren't they? But scratch a little, and lo and behold! There's a real live human being. Imagine that!

Like Surfing, Like Skiing, Like Skateboarding, LIKE...SNOWBOARDING!

This is a more than casual but not quite in-depth comparison of SPORTS. I'm not getting into cultures, style or language. I'd rather not venture into the snowboarder versus skier debate. Young versus old, baggy pants versus neon tights stuff. That's all just a load of superficial bunk.

LIKE SURFING

I can see how people can call snowboarding snow surfing. At a glance, you see a youngish, surfer-type guy or gal standing surfer-like on a board, whizzing and twirling and jumping through the snow. Kinda like a surfer whizzes and twirls and jumps (well, sometimes) on the face of a wave.

They certainly seem to belong to the same family/ culture/genre. Surfers are snowboarders (like me) and snowboarders are surfers. In most surf shops within a half day's drive, you'll find snowboarding stuff. Contests are held these days that feature both sports (there's a long drive in between events.) Both sports are naturalistic, individualistic, thrilling, young (thinking) and daring. Both require balance, flexibility, quick reflexes, and a strong pair of legs.

But the physics of the sports are uh . . . quite different. In surfing, a rider slides and rides a moving mass of water on a strapless surfboard. You turn and burn by shifting weight and working with the actions of the wave.

In snowboarding, a rider slides down a snow-covered slope due to gravity and the planing surface of the board which is strapped on. You turn and burn by shifting weight and working in concert with the edges of your snowboard.

It's this 'edges thing' that beats up so many novices when they first try. Sure edges come into play in surfing, but not like in snowboarding. Snowboarding is all edges. And there are very specific ways edges work in snow that you gotta learn.

LIKE SKIING

Skiing is a similar sport. There, I've said it. Go ahead and throw the turnips. I don't care if skiers don't look the same, or talk the same, or act the same. The one big difference I see in the sports is that skiers strap two slats on, and we strap on one. So techniques are different.

But both sports use exactly the same physics at exactly the same places. Both involve sliding down snow covered slopes on planing surfaces because of gravity. Both involve turning in and out of the fall line, using the edges of their planing surfaces. Edge control is the key for kicks, and the ultimate goal for all technique outside of acrobatics.

If you know how to ski, you have an advantage. Unlike other blank slate novices, you have a feel for sliding on snow, edging on the slopes, and soaking wet gloves.

LIKE SKATEBOARDING

Skateboarding has had a tremendous influence on snowboarding. So many of the acrobatics are inspired by the sport on wheels, especially those performed in the half-pipe. The ranks of snowboarders are replete with sidewalk shredders, including the guy who just may have started it all, Tom Sims. Of course, the stance is similar and the act of skating downhill shares the 'gravity feed' aspect of downhill snowboarding. That is, gravity provides the pull, hence the propulsion on an inclined surface.

But skateboarders don't dig the edges of their boards into the asphalt to make a turn. They shift their weight and work with the special trucking devices that the wheels are attached to. Skateboards roll. They do not slide.

Again the demands of edge control aren't part of the physics of this sport.

So? Snowboarding is somewhat like skiing and not so much like surfing or skateboarding. As a student it's best to approach the learning of snowboarding without the baggage of similarities. Snowboarding is its own thing and best approached without expectations.

The Pioneers

These two gentlemen are on
everyone's most influential list.
(Presented in alphabetical order.)

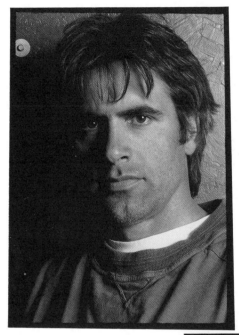

Jake Burton Carpenter

At 39, a legend in his prime. Competitor, innovator, marketeer, and businessman. He started making Burton Snowboards in a woodshop in 1977 and never stopped. Or gave up the lead. You could say his company is a cornerstone of the snowboarding world.

Tom Sims

In 1963 he built the first verifiable snowboard. His company is one of the world's leading manufacturers, innovators and influences in snowboarding today. What's going on at Sims is more often than not what will be going on in snowboarding soon.

Photo: J. Cassinus

HISTORY

Snowboarding is a very, very, young sport . . . The first verifiable snowboard was built in 1963.

Manufacturing of boards and organized competition didn't begin until around 1970.

It wasn't until 1982 that the first really big contest was held and covered by the major media.

It wasn't until 1986 that the first snowboarding instruction was offered at a ski resort.

Although resorts had gradually opened their doors since the '70s, it wasn't until 1989 that these major ski areas opened theirs: Squaw Valley (California), Mammoth Mountain (California), Vail (Colorado), Sun Valley (Idaho) and Snowbird (Utah).

Snowboarding is still largely influenced by the very names that invented it: Tom Sims, Dimitrije Milovich, Jake Burton Carpenter, Chuck Barfoot, Paul Graves . . . And they aren't old men.

A young sport, indeed. With a huge, huge future.

Here's a year by year summation of major events graciously provided by *TransWorld SNOWboarding Magazine*. Itself only six years old.

SNOWBOARDING HISTORICAL TIME LINE

1929—According to a letter sent to *TransWorld SNOWboarding Magazine*, M. J. "Jack" Burtchett cuts out a piece of plywood, secures his feet to it with horse reins and clothesline, and surfs the first winter wave. Although he doesn't have a copy of the board or any record, his claim would make him the first person on a snowboard. Even predating skateboards. Any takers?

1963—Tom Sims makes his first "skiboard" for an eighth grade project in New Jersey.

1965—Sherman Poppen invents the *Snurfer* for his kids by bolting two skis together. He later organizes competitions for *Snurfers* at the Pando Ski Area in Rockford, Michigan.

1969—Mike Doyle develops the monoski which is a forerunner to the alternative ski concept.

1970—Inspired by sliding on cafeteria trays in upstate New York, east coast surfer Dimitrije Milovich starts developing snowboards, "... based on surfboard design with a rudimentary idea of how skis work." Milovich claims that the boards had metal edges, which would be fifteen years prior to when they were first believed to have been used.

1971—Milovich is granted a patent for his snowboard design so that he can sell the idea to ski companies. The patent doesn't expire until 1988. Milovich declines from enforcing the patent with other companies.

1969–1972—Bob Webber spends several years trying to obtain a patent for his early "skiboard" design. The patent is granted in 1972. He later sells the patent to Jake Burton Carpenter on August 17, 1990.

1975—Dimitrije Milovich establishes Winterstick Snowboards in Utah. The metal edges that were featured on his earlier boards are removed. "We didn't need them. We were riding in powder over our heads," Milovich now says. Milovich also develops a swallow-tail board based on the same design in surfboards. One year later he gets a patent on a double edged design.

- Milovich and Winterstick are written up in the March issue of *Newsweek* and have a two-page photo spread in *Powder*, giving snowboarding early national exposure.

1977—Mike Olsen builds his first snowboard in junior high woodshop. He continues to modify boards and in 1984 starts Gnu Snowboards.

- Jake Burton Carpenter moves to Stratton Mountain, Vermont. He works as a bartender at night and designs the prototypes for what will later be Burton Snowboards during the day. Like Sims, he claims to have been modifying *Snurfers* since high school.
- Milovich obtains a written confirmation from Petit-Morey and Kendall Insurance (the insurance brokers for America's ski resorts) that snowboards are in fact covered under regular ski liability. This proves that resort acceptance is based on the mountain manager's preference, just as suspected.
- Bob Webber designs the "yellow banana" polyethylene molded bottom and Tom Sims tacks on the Lonnie Toft skate deck to make the first production "Skiboard" under the Sims name.

1978—Milovich says that by this year he sells *Wintersticks* in 11 different foreign countries.

- In Santa Barbara, surfer/skater Chuck Barfoot develops a fiberglass prototype snowboard. He and Bob Webber take it out to Utah for a test run. Barfoot later goes on to design boards with Tom Sims.

1979—Although Milovich's designs never sold to ski companies as intended, the Hexel ski company produces a double-edged ski and a swallow-tail ski. This is the first evidence of ski design copying snowboarding design.

- At the annual *Snurfer* contest held in Michigan, sponsored *Snurfer* pro Paul Graves puts on a freestyle demo and wows the crowd by doing four sliding 360s, dropping down on one knee for part of the course, and dismounting off his board at the finish with a front flip.

  At the same event, Jake Burton Carpenter tries to enter on his own equipment. There are protests about his non-*Snurfer* snowboard design. Paul Graves and others stand up for Jake's right to race and an open division is created which Jake enters and wins.

- Paul Graves rides a *Snurfer* in the first TV commercial to feature snowboarding. The LaBatt's Beer spot runs four years in Canada and the northern USA.

1979–80—*Skateboarder* and *Action Now* magazines both print early features on the rising sport of snowboarding.

1980—Both Burton Snowboards and Winterstick Snowboards utilize a P-Tex base on their prototype boards, introducing ski technology to the industry.

1981—After working on early developments at Sims, Chuck Barfoot leaves to form his own company.

- Modern competitive snowboarding begins with a small contest held in April at Ski Cooper in Leadville, Colorado.

1982—Paul Graves organizes the National Snowboarding Championships at Suicide Six Ski Area in Woodstock, Vermont. A slalom and a downhill event are featured. Racers in the downhill are clocked at speeds in excess of 60 mph.

This is the first time riders nationwide have competed against each other including rivals Tom Sims and Jake Burton Carpenter. Burton team rider Doug Bouton wins first overall.

The contest also features the first amateur division. It's the last time *Snurfers* and snowboards race together. The contest draws media coverage from the likes of *Sports Illustrated, NBC Today* and *Good Morning America.*

1983—Jake Burton Carpenter organizes the National Snowboarding Championships in the spring at Snow Valley, Vermont. Tom Sims then goes home and holds the inaugural World Snowboarding Championships at Soda Springs Ski Bowl in the Lake Tahoe area. This is the first contest to have a half-pipe event.

- Jeff Grell designs the first highback binding, enabling boards to be ridden effectively on hardpack. The bindings were first used on Flite Snowboards but later developed for Sims Snowboards. Grell makes the history books but never sees any money from his innovation.

1985—*Skateboarder* covers the World Championships at Soda Springs. This is some of the first magazine exposure for a snowboarding event.

- In January, Mt. Baker hosts the first Mt. Baker Legendary Banked Slalom which becomes a competitive mainstay. Tom Sims wins.

- *Absolutely Radical*, the first magazine exclusively about snowboarding, appears in March. Six months later the name changes to *International Snowboard Magazine.*
- Skater Marty Jiminez writes *TransWorld SKATEboarding*'s first snowboard article in the April issue.
- Metal edges are introduced on the Sims 1500 FE and Burton Performer models. This ends the era of surfing-influenced fin design once and for all. Snowboard design begins to incorporate ski technology.
- Sims Snowboards introduces the first signature model snowboard in their winter line, bearing Terry Kidwell's name. The Kidwell is also the first freestyle board with a rounded tail.
- Mike Olsen's Gnu Snowboards are the first to be marketed as carving boards--upon which turns can be made more precisely with less sliding.

1986—Europeans begin to organize their own regional events, such as the Swiss Championships in St. Moritz.

- The Swiss winner of some of those European races, Jose Fernandes, comes to America with an asymmetrical board, the forerunner to today's 'asym' production models. The board is made by his sponsor, Hooger Booger.
- The World Snowboarding Championships, or the World's, as it has become known, relocates from Soda Springs to Breckenridge, Colorado. The March event draws big money from Swatch and generates the most national interest to date. Fran Richards, Paul Alden, and Dave Alden convince the Breckenridge management that the half-pipe is not a high-speed event.
- Stratton Mountain in Vermont becomes the first resort to offer organized snowboarding instruction.

- Sims Snowboards is licensed by Vision in December.

1986–1987—With a lace-up ski-boot inner bladder, Burton Snowboards produces what will become the standard design for soft-boot snowboarding.

1987—Chuck Barfoot and his company introduce the first twin-tip freestyle shape with an identical nose and tail. The board is designed by Canadians Neil Daffern, Ken and Dave Achenbach.

- Europeans host their own World Championships in January at Livigno, Italy, and St. Moritz, Switzerland. This event is not to be confused with the other World Championships, held at Breckenridge, Colorado later the same year.
- The day after the second Breckenridge World's in March, Paul Alden and a collection of riders and manufacturers form the North American Snowboard Association (NASA). The acronym is later changed to NASBA because NASA is already taken. The association's main goal is to work with the Snowboard European Association (SEA) to create a unified world cup tour.
- A host of early snowboarders, including Dave Alden, pen the first PSIA manual for snowboard instructors.
- *TransWorld SNOWboarding Magazine* publishes its first issue in the fall.
- In September, Wrigley's Chewing Gum utilizes snowboarding in a national commercial. Craig Kelly, Bert LaMar, Tom Burt, and Jim Zellers appear in an aerial romp filmed by Greg Stump.

1987–1988—The first World Cup is held throughout the season with two events in Europe and two in the United States. The circuit also introduces major corporate sponsorship (O'Neill, Suzuki, and Swatch) into the competitive arena.

1988—Veteran surf company Ocean Pacific (OP) warms up to snowboarding by developing their own line of winter clothing. Other surf companies soon follow and capitalize on the crossover between the two sports.

- Further action sport involvement comes when surf and skate manufacturer G&S enters the market. By 1990, G&S exits the snowboard market.
- While the two major snowboard manufacturers, Burton and Sims, battle over Craig Kelly in court, he is ordered by a federal judge not to ride any products bearing any logo other than Sims. Kelly then starts riding boards with no logo. The restraining order is later reversed in court and Kelly signs a long-term deal with Burton.
- Former amateur surf promoter Chuck Allen incorporates the United States Amateur Snowboarding Association (USASA) in July with a $500 donation from *TransWorld SNOWboarding Magazine*. USASA is the first governing body exclusively for competitive amateur snowboarding.

1989—Earl A. Miller, an engineer and inventor from Utah, produces a releasable snowboard binding, but the technology has yet to hit the mainstream.

- Just in time for the coming winter, most of the major ski resorts that had previously resisted snowboarding succumb. They include Squaw Valley, California; Mammoth Mountain, California; Vail, Colorado; Sun Valley, Idaho; and Snowbird, Utah.
- OP continues to delve into the snowboarding market by expanding their popular OP Pro of Surfing to include the OP Pro of Snowboarding. The contest is held at June Mountain, California.
- The first National Collegiate Championships

are held in December at Stratton Mountain, Vermont. Soon, college teams and clubs sprout like weeds throughout the country.

1990—Jake Burton Carpenter buys the patent for the "skiboard" from its designer Bob Webber. The industry fears he will make them pay royalties on all board sales. But Burton never pursues the issue, making the patent a moot point.

- The USASA holds their premiere National Championships in February, at Snow Valley, California. The worst snowstorm of the decade hits just before the event and closes all roads to Big Bear. Amateur snowboarders from all over the country are left stranded. A rescue caravan of locals led by USASA president Chuck Allen sneaks the competitors past the police barricades and gets them to the contest on time.
- In June, Breckenridge Ski Corporation announces plans to house the Snowboarding Hall of Fame, with artifacts from the sports not-so-distant past.
- Santa Cruz Skateboards' owner Rich Novak starts producing a line of snowboards. Other skate companies like H-Street decide to test the waters with their own board and clothing designs.
- Vail Ski Resort tries a new approach by developing an inbounds obstacle area called a "snowboard park." The area is intended to cater to a growing snowboard market and other resorts quickly follow suit.

1991—By now, the pro surfer/pro skater crossover to snowboarding is prevalent. Skaters Steve Caballero and Lance Mountain have been riding since the early '80s. Tony Hawk, Kevin Staab and Joe Johnson have been riding for years. Recent convert Mike Youssefpour puts in slope time as well. Surf stand-outs like Gary Elkerton and Noah Budroe bite the snowboarding bait, and most other pro surfers ride regularly, or have tried it.

- After a lengthy court dispute over the Sims name, Tom Sims wins back the licensing rights from Vision in February. Vision begins production under its own name and Tom resumes making a new Sims line.
- The OP Wintersurf contest held in February pits pro surfers and snowboarders against each other in a surf contest at Huntington Beach, and a snowboard obstacle course/race at Bear Mountain. Top international pro surfer Gary Elkerton scores the win, proving it's a lot harder to learn how to surf than snowboard.

1993—The International Snowboard Federation holds its first official Snowboard World Championships in Ischgl, Austria. Kevin Delaney and Michele Taggart win the combined titles.

SPECIAL NOTE

Like any history, this time line by *TransWorld SNOWboarding* is subject to debate, review and revision. Please take it for what it is — a superb starting point and, as far as I know, the best snowboarding history to date. Many thanks to the dedicated staff of *TransWorld SNOWboarding* for allowing me to reproduce their invaluable contribution to the sport.

GLOSSARY

There is an absolutely dizzying array of terms and expressions in snowboarding. Most of the really bizzare ones refer to the advanced manueveres, which are invented on a daily basis. This list includes all you really need to know.

A

AIR—The space achieved between board and snow by leaping, jumping, etc.

ALPINE—Refers to downhill snowboarding involving speed and carving turns. Alpine boards are built 'stiff' to maximize speed and to hold an edge during turns.

ARTIFICIAL SNOW—The 'real' snow made by machines at ski areas in order to extend the skiing\snowboarding season.

ASYMMETRICAL—Refers to snowboard design that is asymmetrical in shape. The angle off the 'asym' is determined by the position of the rider's feet on the board.

B

BARNEY—Person with all the social skills of Barney Fife, Deputy Sheriff.

BONKING—Hitting something while riding a snowboard.

BUTTPLANT—Falling on one's butt.

C

CARVE—A turn that is true to the radius of a snowboard's sidecut.

CATCHING AN EDGE—Digging the downhill edge of a snowboard into the snow while descending a slope. Usually results in a head- or buttplant.

EDGES—The sides of a snowboard.

FAKIE—Riding a snowboard backwards.

FALL LINE—The path of least resistance down a given slope. The path a ball would take if released at the top.

FREESTYLE—Refers to snowboarding activity that involves quick turns and trick manuevers. Freestyle boards are generally twin-tipped and easy to turn (loose).

GOOFY FOOT—Riding a snowboard with the right foot forward.

GROOMING—Preparing the snow at a ski area with 'snowcats'. Usually a night time activity, snocats press down snow, break up ice and fill in dips. May also involve the manufacture of 'artificial snow'.

HALF-PIPE—A trough dug out of a slope in order for snowboarders to perform aerial manuevers off its sides.

HARDPACK—A snow condition where old snow has settled into a 'hard' mass. Not an ideal surface to ride on.

HARD-SHELL BOOT—A snowboarding boot made of hard plastic. Provides maximum support for alpine/racing snowboarding (usually) with plate bindings.

HEADPLANT—Falling on your head.

HIGHBACK BINDINGS—The type of snowboard bindings used for freestyle riding with soft boots. The 'high'-backs provide necessary ankle support.

ICE—A snow condition where the slope has frozen into a hard sheet. A very difficult surface to snowboard on.

LIFT—The chairlift at a ski area.

MOGULS—The 'bumps' made by the tracks of skiers\snowboarders over a period of time on the face of a slope.

MONOSKI—The single ski concept developed by Mike Doyle in 1969.

PLATE BINDING—A type of snowboarding binding used for racing or alpine riding with hard-shell boots.

POWDER—Usually a freshly fallen snow condition with relatively little moisture content. Riders tend to sink or settle in powder as they ride, requiring specific riding techniques. A difficult yet deeply satisfying surface for experts.

RACING—Downhill snowboarding involving maximum speed and carving turns. A step up from alpine snowboarding in these catagories. Racing snowboards are the thinnest and 'stiffest' of snowboards.

REGULAR FOOT—Riding a snowboard with the left foot forward.

SHRED—To ride a snowboard (or anything, really) very, very well.

SIDECUT—The concave edge design of a snowboard.

SKIBOARD—The name or label applied to early snowboards developed by Tom Sims and Bob Webber, among others.

SKID—To travel down a slope sideways. The length of the board is at right angles to the fall line.

SLALOM—A downhill race where snowboarders or skiers turn around staggered flags or poles.

SLUSH—A snow condition where the sun has melted the slopes to a slurpy-like consistancy. Not usually a good surface to snowboard on.

SNOWBOARD PARK—An area set aside at ski areas/resorts for special snowboarding activity. Usually includes a half-pipe and various 'playground furniture' to bonk and jump over, etc.

SNOCATS—The big grooming machines at ski areas. Their tank-like treads mash down snow into a suitable surface for skiing\snowboarding.

SNURFER—The forerunner of the snowboard. Invented in 1965 by Sherman Poppen. The Snurfer was more or less a wide, wooden ski with a rope handle attached to the nose.

SOFT BOOT—A flexable snowboarding boot designed for freestyle riding with highback bindings. Usually has inner and outer boot. Both lace up and are made of pliable material.

STOMP PAD—The pad between bindings on a snowboard. Here a rider can rest his\her unbound foot while gliding.

SWALLOW TAIL—An early snowboard tail design lifted from surfboard design. Tail is shaped into two points.

(T)

360—Spinning or turning 360 degrees.

TRANSFERING EDGES—Turning. Refers to the act of shifting the downhill edge of a snowboard to an uphill edge while changing direction. And vice versa.

TRAVERSE—To angle sideways across the face of a slope and its fall line.

TWIN-TIP—A snowboard with both an up-turned nose and tail enabling the rider to ride forwards or backwards. Associated with freestyle riding.

NOTES

A SPECIAL THANKS...

Robin Niehaus — The guy in all the shots has been snowboarding for five seasons. He has also cut a hit record (absolutely true), managed a surf shop, surfed and skated for ten years and will graduate from San Diego State University with a degree in business management. His greatest achievement, however, was teaching me how to snowboard.

Craig McClain — The guy who took the shots is one of the leading photographers in Southern California and is gaining national recognition for his computer graphics as well. An avid sportsman, Craig shreds (shreds?) in golf, tennis, and skiing. Yes. He knows how to snowboard.

Snow Valley Ski Resort — Site of the legendary 1990 USASA National Championships and home base for one of the finest staffs anywhere. Snow Valley is the oldest and largest resort in the San Bernardino Mountains, with over 230 acres of skiing/snowboarding terrain, 35 trails and 13 chair lifts. The renowned "monster" half-pipe is a magnet for Southern California snowboarders.

Located just 90 minutes from LA, Snow Valley is ideal for day trips and offers various packages that include lodging for those who wish to stay longer. Rentals and expert instruction available. For more information call (909) 867-2751.

 Snow Valley is operated under a special permit from the U.S. Forest Service and is located in the San Bernardino National Forest.

NOTES

RESOURCES

SNOWBOARD/SKI/SURF SHOPS

The best source for information, gear, etc. is a snowboard shop, which can often be found combined with a ski and/or surf shop depending on your locale. Shops should be able to provide you with the best local information about:

- Snowboarding areas
- Snowboarding camps
- Snowboarding schools/lessons
- Snow conditions
- Snowboarding contests
- Snowboarding organizations

Shops also provide:

- Snowboards
- Snowboarding gear
- Snowboarders to talk to
- Snowboarding magazines and literature

Snowboard/ski shops are littered around ski areas, of course, and can be found in major cities within a half-day's drive to the mountains. Beach cities may have combined surf and snowboard shops. Just check the yellow pages.

SNOWBOARDING MAGAZINES

In the USA their are two big ones: *TransWorld SNOWboarding* and *Snowboarder*. Both celebrate the sport with HOT pix and graphics that make you wanna snowboard NOW. Articles about areas, riders, equipment, issues and history are generally well written and hip (very).

TransWorld SNOWboarding
353 Airport Road
Oceanside, CA 92054

Snowboarder
33046 Calle Aviador
San Juan Capistrano, CA 92675

TELEVISION

Watch the *Prime Ticket Cable Network, ESPN,* and *MTV* for occasional snowboarding programs. They aren't prolific but they're there sometimes. Also the *ISF* (International Snowboard Federation) *Media Network* has channel access in 67 countries. Check out your local listings.

VIDEOS

Lots of videos out now showing the very best riders doing the impossible. Find them at the shops and the stores next to or around ski areas.

SNOWBOARDING ORGANIZATIONS

At this time, this is what I've got. Understand that since the sport is so young this organization business can change.

▶ **International Snowboard Federation**
This is considered by many to be the sanctioning body for the following organizations. Many roads lead and depart from here. Information about all of them can be obtained by calling or writing:

ISF
PO Box 477
Vail, Colorado 81658
(303) 949-5473

Professional
- Professional Snowboarders Association of North America (PSA North America)
- Professional Snowboarders Association of Europe (PSA Europe)
- Professional Snowboarders Association of Japan (PSA Japan)

Amateur
- International Snowboard Association of North America (ISA North America)
- International Snowboard Association of Europe (ISA Europe)
- Canadian Snowboard Federation (CSF)
- United States Amateur Snowboarding Association (USASA)

▶ **The United States Ski Association (USSA)**
The USSA has its own amateur competition program.

USSA
P.O. Box 100
Park City, Utah 84060
(801) 649-9090

NOTES

BIBLIOGRAPHY

Berry, I. William. *The Great American Ski Book*. New York, New York: Charles Scribner's Sons, 1982.

Campbell, Stu. *The Way to Ski!* Tucson, Arizona: The Body Press, 1986.

Fodor's Skiing in North America. New York, New York: Fodor's Travel Publications, Inc., 1989.

Gamma, Carl. *The Handbook of Skiing*. New York, New York: Alfred A. Knopf, Inc., 1989.

Masia, Seth. *Ski Magazine's Managing the Mountain*. New York, New York: Simon and Schuster, 1992.

Snowboarder Magazine. San Juan Capistrano, California: Surfer Publications, Inc.

TransWorld SNOWboarding Magazine. Oceanside, California: Imprimatur, Inc.

INDEX

LEARN HOW TO SURF!

ENDORSED BY **MAJOR SURFING ASSOCIATIONS**

Surfer's Start-UP

A Beginner's Guide to Surfing

Doug Werner

Available at Bookstores
& Surf Shops Nationwide